2

EGYPTIAN DYNASTIES

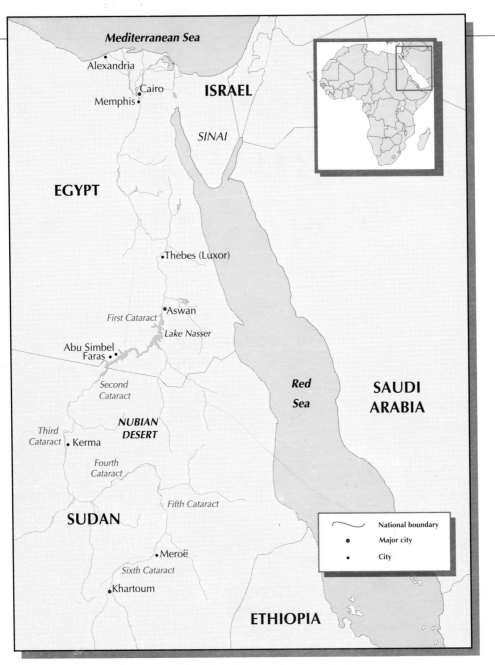

The popular fascination with ancient Egypt continues to this day.

~African Civilizations~

EGYPTIAN DYNASTIES

Joyce L. Haynes

A First Book

Franklin Watts
A Division of Grolier Publishing
New York / London / Hong Kong / Sydney
Danbury, Connecticut

Cover photograph copyright ©: Erich Lessing/Art Resource

Photographs copyright ©: Trip/Trip/The Viesti Collection, Inc.: pp. 7, 28, 49; Roger Wood/Corbis: pp. 8, 30, 38; Richard and Mary Magruder/Viesti Associates, Inc.: p. 11; 1992, Bill Gallery/Viesti Associates, Inc.: pp. 12, 36; Joe Viesti/Viesti Associates, Inc.: p. 15; Gianni Dagli Orti/Corbis: p. 16; Richard Nowitz/Corbis: pp. 18, 24; Joyce Haynes: pp. 21, 26, 46, 52, 54, 58; Trip/T. Bognar/The Viesti Collection, Inc.: p. 22; Trip/P. Mitchell/ The Viesti Collection, Inc.: p. 41; Jack Fields/Corbis: pp. 43, 45.

Library of Congress Cataloging-in-Publication Data

Haynes, Joyce L. (Joyce Louise), 1947-
    Egyptian dynasties / Joyce Haynes. — 1st ed.
        p.   cm. — (African civilizations)
    Includes bibliographical references (p. 62) and index.
    Summary: A survey of the history and culture of the North African
Egyptian dynasties.
    ISBN 0-531-20280-1
    1. Egypt—Civilization—To 332 B.C.—Juvenile literature. 2. Egypt—
Civilization—To 332 B.C.   I. Title.   II. Series
DT61.H39   1998
932—dc21   97-29390
                                                              CIP
                                                              AC

Copyright © 1998 by The Rosen Publishing Group, Inc.
All rights reserved. Published simultaneously in Canada
Printed in the United States of America
1 2 3 4 5 6 7 8 9 10 R 05 04 03 02 01 00 99 98

CONTENTS

INTRODUCTION 6

1 THE PHARAOHS 14

2 RELIGION 34

3 EVERYDAY LIFE 48

4 WRITING AND ART 56

TIMELINE 60

GLOSSARY 61

FOR FURTHER READING 62

INDEX 63

INTRODUCTION

Egypt lies in the northeast corner of Africa. This great ancient center of civilization is 96 percent desert. Without the waters of the Nile River, the earliest Egyptians could not have survived or developed a great civilization. Apart from providing drinkable water, the Nile allowed the Egyptians to water crops, transport goods, fish, and hunt the animals and birds that lived in the marshes along its banks.

Ancient Egyptians depended on the flooding of the Nile River each summer. When the floodwater receded it left behind a rich deposit of silt along the banks of the river. Because the soil was so full of nutrients, Egyptian fruits and vegetables were—and still are—large and delicious. They are even mentioned in the Bible.

Egyptian fruits and vegetables are famous throughout the world, even as they were in ancient times.

The Nile was essential for travel and transportation of cargo as well as for farming. A view of the Nile near Aswan.

The Nile flows northward, entering Egypt in the south and emptying into the Mediterranean Sea on Egypt's northern edge. The Nile flows from south to north because the land in the south is higher than the land in the north. That is why, in ancient times and even today, the southern part of Egypt is called Upper Egypt and the northern part is Lower Egypt.

The smooth flow of the Nile in Egypt made it the superhighway of travel and trade in ancient times. The current of the Nile and a little rowing easily carried boats northward. To travel south, it was necessary to raise a sail to catch the wind that blew from north to south. The cool breezes on the river and the view of the lush green marshes on either side of the Nile made river travel far more pleasant than walking along the desert paths or bumping along on the back of a donkey.

The Nile, however, is easy to sail only as far as the city of Aswan. Here, at the southern border of ancient Egypt, the gentle flow of the Nile turns into rapids that rush between large granite boulders. These rapids are called *cataracts*. In modern times a great dam was built on the Nile at Aswan. Today, the water that once flooded the banks of the Nile each year is now stored and controlled by this dam.

Ancient Egypt was ruled by pharaohs (FARE-ohs). The pharaohs aimed to pass the throne on to someone in their own family, usually a son but sometimes a brother, wife, or daughter. When power was passed on within one family, without a takeover or break, that family and its rule are known as a *dynasty*.

Breaks between Egyptian dynasties are called *Intermediate Periods*.

Most experts agree that thirty different dynasties ruled between 3000 B.C., when Egyptians were first united under one ruler, and 332 B.C., when the Greeks conquered Egypt. During this entire period of almost three thousand years, the all-powerful pharaohs made sure that Egyptian culture remained remarkably stable. Key elements of ancient Egyptian culture were: rule by pharaohs, religious beliefs that included the worship of many gods and the belief in an *afterlife*, and the Egyptian system of writing, using characters known as *hieroglyphs*.

Egyptologists—scholars who study ancient Egypt—are able to learn a great deal from hieroglyphic writings and Egyptian art and architecture. These provide much evidence about life in ancient Egypt and about its pharaohs.

Egypt's power stemmed not only from having strong rulers who headed up a centralized system of government. Egypt was also self-sufficient in food, it manufactured and exported such products as linen, and it imported a variety of products from neighboring regions, including gold and ivory from Nubia,

Temple at Abu Simbel built by Ramesses II, or Ramesses the Great, in about 1250 B.C. for the goddess Hathor and Ramesses' queen, Nefertari

Hieroglyphs fell into disuse in about the fourth century, and their meaning was lost. After they were decoded in the nineteenth century, hieroglyphs revealed fascinating information about ancient Egypt.

which lay farther up the Nile River. At times, Egypt's military forces conquered neighboring territories, including Nubia.

After the Greeks, and later the Romans, conquered Egypt, Egyptian culture was drawn more and more closely into the Mediterranean world of the Greeks and Romans. Hieroglyphs fell into disuse shortly after A.D. 394, and their meaning was soon forgotten. For many centuries nobody could read the inscriptions on Egyptian temples and statues. For this reason little was known about the mysterious culture of ancient Egypt.

Finally, in 1822, a French scholar named Jean François Champollion began to decode hieroglyphs. His breakthrough came while he was working on an ancient inscription. Called the Rosetta Stone, it contained the same information in Greek, hieroglyphs, and in a form of phonetic hieroglyphs. By comparing the hieroglyphs to the Greek, which could be easily read, Champollion translated the first hieroglyphs.

Since then, our ability to read hieroglyphs has opened the door to a deeper understanding of this remarkable civilization. Thanks to the ancient Egyptians who wrote about themselves, we have firsthand information about their times.

THE PHARAOHS

People lived in Egypt for many thousands of years. But it was not until about 3000 B.C. that the Egyptians were united by one pharaoh.

The word pharaoh comes from the ancient Egyptian *per-iah*, which means "great house," and was used to refer to the royal palace. A pharaoh was traditionally a king, but rarely a queen.

Pharaohs were regarded as living gods and played a key role in the religious life of ancient Egypt. They inspired and coordinated the building of such monumental structures as the pyramids, the royal tombs in the Valley of the Kings, and gigantic temple complexes, which include the

Many pharaohs of the New Kingdom were buried in the Valley of the Kings.

famous temples of Karnak and Luxor. Priests, who were also the scholars of ancient Egypt, compiled lists of pharaohs and the dates of their reigns. Unfortunately no two lists agree, and this leads to much debate among Egyptologists today. For convenience scholars now divide the history of ancient Egypt into the Old Kingdom, Middle Kingdom, New Kingdom, and Late Period. Between these kingdoms were a number of Intermediate Periods, when Egypt was ruled by many different warring kings or even by foreign rulers.

Relief carving of Ramesses II killing one of his enemies

The pharaohs led Egypt through many political achievements and led its armies on conquering expeditions that greatly expanded Egypt's boundaries. At times Egypt's territory extended all the way to the Euphrates River in the Near East and far south into Nubia in present-day Sudan.

The time of the great warrior pharaohs and the greatest expansion was during the New Kingdom. Soon after this great empire-building period, however, Egypt gradually declined. It was conquered by several foreign powers. The Egyptians sometimes regained power for a brief time, but by the sixth century B.C. they were already fatally weakened. Under the Greeks and Romans, Egyptian culture declined.

The fame of many Egyptian pharaohs survived, however. Because the ancient Egyptians believed that to say a person's name helped him to live on, we are "giving life" to these ancient pharaohs as we continue to talk about them, write about them, and show their art in museums.

CHUFU, THE PYRAMID BUILDER

The greatest pyramid builders of ancient Egypt were the pharaohs of Dynasty Four (2575-2465 B.C.). King Chufu (KHOO-fu) created the largest pyramid in Egypt. It is one of the Three Great Pyramids at Giza, which are regarded today as one

The Three Great Pyramids at Giza, with man and camel in foreground

of the Seven Wonders of the Ancient World.

Chufu's pyramid was taller than a fifty-story building and contained more than 2.3 million blocks of limestone. As soon as he became pharaoh, Chufu ordered work to begin on building his pyramid. The pyramid was to be his burial place, so it had to be finished before Chufu died. The construction took twenty-three years.

The pyramids were built by hardworking Egyptians, although Hollywood movies often show them being built by slaves. Between July and October each year, when the Nile flooded, thousands of Egyptians who normally worked in the fields were unemployed. During this time the pharaohs hired crews of men to build their pyramids, temples, and tombs.

The government paid the laborers with bread, beer, and other foods and supplies. The teams of workers on Chufu's pyramid carved their names into the limestone *quarries* where they cut stones. Two interesting names found there are "The Victorious Gang" and "The Craftsmen of Chufu." The workers' village was near the Giza pyramids. Recent excavations at their village have uncovered the village bakery, workers' homes, pottery, and fishhooks.

HATSHEPSUT

One of the most remarkable women of ancient Egypt was Queen Hatshepsut (HAHT-shep-suit), who ruled from 1473 to 1458 B.C. She was the first woman to rule as a pharaoh.

When Hatshepsut's husband, Pharaoh Thutmose (THOOT- moze) II, died, the throne was left to one of Thutmose's sons, Thutmose III. Since he was only a child at the time, Hatshepsut, his stepmother, officially became his co-ruler. She was the dominant ruler from the start. The term "queen" in ancient Egypt meant "wife of the king." Hatshepsut was the first woman to call herself "king" and wear the traditional costume of male pharaohs: a short, pleated kilt, or *shendjet*, a false beard, and a crown with a uraeus, or rearing cobra, on the front.

Hatshepsut built many monuments. As was the custom, these were decorated with images of the ruler. She sometimes had herself portrayed wearing the king's costume and with a man's body. If she had been shown wearing a dress the people would have regarded her as a mortal woman, rather than a living god.

One of Hatshepsut's greatest monuments is her temple, located at Deir el Bahri. The layout of the temple is impressive. Each of its three stories was placed on a separate terrace. The front of each story was lined with columns through which the halls could be entered. The area in front of the temple was landscaped with trees. The long walkway

Relief carving on an obelisk at the Temple of Karnak. Hatshepsut, shown with a man's body, wears a *shendjet* and kneels before Amun who places the pharaoh's crown on her head.

Queen Hatshepsut's temple at Deir el Bahri, on the western bank of the Nile at Luxor

approaching the temple was lined with statues of Hatshepsut. It must have been a wonderful sight in the desert. Inside the temple were beautiful *relief carvings* recording events of Hatshepsut's reign.

Hatshepsut's chief architect, named Senmut, is credited with overseeing her building activities. He played a special role in Hatshepsut's life because he was also the nurse and caretaker of her daughter,

Neferure. Many statues show the young princess seated on his lap.

Hatshepsut and her daughter disappeared from the official Egyptian records in about 1458 B.C., when Thutmose III took full control of the throne. After he had ruled for nearly fifty years, he had many of Hatshepsut's monuments and sculptures destroyed. Egyptologists now believe that he did this to erase her memory. He did not want the Egyptian people to regard his own son as linked to Hatshepsut in any way. Rather, he wanted to emphasize that his son, Amenhotep II, who would soon become king, was a direct descendant of King Thutmose II.

The famous *obelisks* called Cleopatra's Needles that now stand in London and New York were in fact first erected in Egypt by Thutmose III. Just as Thutmose attempted to erase the name of Hatshepsut, so too has his connection with these famous monuments been forgotten.

AKHENATON

Akhenaton (AKH-en-AH-ton) ruled from 1350 to 1334 B.C. His name is not mentioned in Egyptian lists of kings. Instead he is called "the enemy,"

Statue of Thutmose III

because he turned Egypt upside down with his radical ideas. He changed Egyptian traditions that had been observed for thousands of years.

He forbade the Egyptians to worship the gods they knew. Instead, he declared that the sun itself was the only god, which he called Aton. Hymns and prayers were written to the new god Aton, such as this example: "Out of yourself alone do you create millions of forms; cities, towns, fields, roads, rivers. Every eye looks at you out there, for you are the sun disc of the daytime, supreme. You shine and the people live, you set and they die. You yourself are lifetime, and through you do they live!"

Akhenaton himself taught Egyptian artists a new way to represent the human figure, with very long, narrow heads, big lips, small shoulders, and full hips.

The end of Akhenaton's life remains a mystery. We do know that once his short reign was over, the Egyptians destroyed all his monuments, tore down his temples, and re-used the blocks of stone.

KING TUTANKHAMUN
King Tutankhamun (TOOT-ankh-amen) reigned from 1333 to 1323 B.C. He came to the throne at

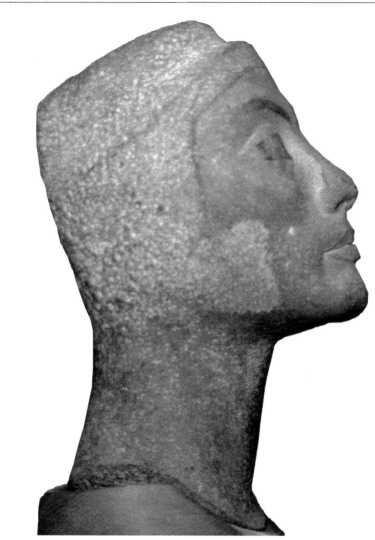

Sculptured head of Akhenaton's queen, Nefertiti

the age of ten. When he died at age nineteen, his tomb had not been completed. Instead he was buried in a very small tomb in the Valley of the Kings—a rocky desert area in Thebes where the pharaohs of the New Kingdom were buried. By this time, pyramids were no longer used as royal tombs, because they were easy to rob. Kings were buried instead in underground tombs, which were dug into the rock hundreds of feet below the surface.

In Tutankhamun's case this burial method preserved the royal treasures. Although thieves did break into his tomb in ancient times, they must have been caught or frightened away, because the treasures buried with the boy king were left intact. They were discovered in 1922 by Howard Carter. Soon the wonderful objects he discovered—and Tutankhamun's name—were world-famous.

The few rooms of Tutankhamun's tomb contained objects most precious to the king: jewelry, gold, *alabaster*, and even his favorite foods, such as dried duck. Statues of guardian jackals and other gods and goddesses were placed there to protect his mummy. The ancient Egyptians believed that the statues and other objects in the tomb would all magically come to life to serve the pharaoh in the next world, the afterlife. Many symbols on Tutankhamun's jewelry represent life after death,

The sarcophagus of Tutankhamun and one of his inner coffins can still be seen in his burial site in the Valley of the Kings.

such as the scarab beetle, which is a symbol of rebirth, and the ankh, a sign that means life.

Among the most impressive objects in Tutankhamun's tomb were three coffins that nested one inside the other. The two outermost were made of gold-covered wood but the innermost was solid gold. On the head of the royal mummy was a solid gold mask, now famous throughout the world as the face of "King Tut." The wonderful works of art from Tutankhamun's tomb were taken to the museum in Egypt's capital city, Cairo. His actual mummy, however, was replaced in its inner coffin and returned to its stone sarcophagus—the stone case that contained the coffins.

RAMESSES II

Ramesses (RA-mass-ees) II, or Ramesses the Great, reigned for sixty-seven years, from 1290 to 1224 B.C. He had thirty-one daughters and outlived twelve of his seventy-nine sons. At age eight Ramesses received a *harem*, and at twelve he was given his own troops to command in Nubia.

Ramesses had many enormous sculptures erected of himself and his name carved into thousands of monuments all over Egypt. He had the names of the previous pharaohs removed from their monuments and replaced with his own. His name was carved so deeply into the stone—up to 2 inches (5 cm) deep—that no one could erase it, and it is still clearly visible on monuments today.

It is fair to say that Ramesses probably had an ego as big as his colossal sculptures. The descriptions of himself that he carved alongside his sculptures state that he is powerful, good-looking, and courageous.

Built in Nubia by Ramesses II, the temple of Abu Simbel was moved to its present position on higher ground overlooking its original site. This preserved it from the waters of the dam built at Aswan in the 1960s.

Ramesses built temples and monuments in every major town in ancient Egypt. At the town of Abu Simbel near the Second Cataract of the Nile, his sculptors carved a gigantic temple into the sandstone cliffs. Inside the temple he is shown as a living god. Four colossal seated statues flank the entrance outside. They are 67 feet tall (20 m)—as tall as a six-story building. Their lips alone are 3 feet (1 m) wide.

CLEOPATRA

The famous Cleopatra was in fact the seventh pharaoh of that name, and she was not Egyptian, but Greek—one of the last of a long line of Greek rulers of Egypt. Greek control of Egypt began in 332 B.C., when Alexander the Great of Macedonia conquered Egypt and much of the Mediterranean world. He founded and named Alexandria, the great coastal city in Egypt.

The Macedonian line of rulers in Egypt ended in 305 B.C., but Greek rule continued under Ptolemy I, one of Alexander's trusted generals. For the next 270 years rulers of the Ptolemaic Dynasty controlled Egypt. Fifteen pharaohs named Ptolemy reigned during that period of time, as well as seven pharaohs named Cleopatra, among many others. This period was filled with palace intrigue, as members of the royal family constantly plotted against relatives who stood between them and the throne. Murders were frequent. More than twenty rulers rapidly succeeded one another.

When Cleopatra VII took the throne at age seventeen, Egypt and the Roman Empire were the two great powers in the Mediterranean world. In 48 B.C. Julius Caesar arrived in Alexandria, met the young queen, and was charmed by her. Seeking absolute power over the ancient Mediterranean world, these two powerful rulers allied their forces. Cleopatra and Caesar became lovers and had a child, who later became Pharaoh Ptolemy XV Caesarion.

Julius Caesar was assassinated in Rome in 44 B.C. His heir, Octavian, and one of his generals, Marc Antony, competed for control. Egypt was to be one of the prizes in the battle between them. This put Cleopatra in a difficult position. She allied with Marc Antony in 41 B.C., and they, too, had children together.

In 31 B.C. Octavian defeated Antony and Cleopatra at the naval battle of Actium, and the two losers committed suicide. This ended the Ptolemaic Dynasty in Egypt and ushered in the Roman rule of Egypt.

Like Hatshepsut, Cleopatra also wanted to be seen as a pharaoh and not a queen. She, too, had herself depicted as a man wearing the royal kilt.

Although Cleopatra is famous today as a legendary beauty, sculptures and coins bearing her image suggest that, in fact, her looks were rather ordinary. This explains why they are not discussed by ancient historians. Instead, writers mention her personality, wit, charm, and intelligence. She is said to have been the only one of the Greek dynasty of the Ptolemies who understood and wrote Egyptian.

It is clear that Cleopatra was a skilled politician. She was able to maintain her rule over Egypt for nearly twenty years.

2 RELIGION

The Egyptians believed that the human body had to be preserved after death. It was the place for the *ka*, a part of a person's spirit, to live during the eternity of the afterlife. The *ka* was considered a person's vital force, and it needed food and water to survive in the afterlife. A person's immortal life was endangered if the *ka* was neglected or if anything happened to the body that housed the *ka*.

Another spirit that lived on was the *ba*, which contained a person's mental and physical abilities. Unlike the *ka*, which never traveled, the *ba* was believed to journey to the heavenly realm during the night and return in the daytime.

MUMMIFICATION

Mumification was the drying process used to prevent the decay of a corpse. All the moisture was dried out of the body by packing it with a sacred blend of salts called natron. The stomach, liver, intestines, and lungs were mummified separately and placed in special jars called canopic jars. The brain was discarded. The Egyptians regarded it as the unimportant "marrow of the skull."

When the body was dry and leathery, it was covered with oils, spices, jewelry, and protective *amulets* and wrapped in linen bandages. The prepared body was waterproofed by applying layers of tree or gum resin, which turned as dark as tar. The word mummy comes from an Arabic word, *mumia*, meaning tar.

OPENING OF THE MOUTH CEREMONY

Egyptians believed that mummification immobilized the spirit of the dead person. To revive the *ba* and *ka*, priests performed the Opening of the Mouth ceremony. One priest acted as the jackal-headed god Anubis. He wore a mask and held the mummy upright, serving as its protector. Meanwhile, the

Egyptian tombs are often painted with scenes that describe the journey of the deceased to the afterlife. The scene at the bottom right, for example, shows the jackal-headed god Anubis attending to the mummy.

chief priest burned incense, poured offerings, and opened the mummy's mouth with a special instrument, shaped like the group of stars now called the Big Dipper. This constellation consists of seven stars that never set. The Egyptians believed that the shape of the instrument would assist their souls in becoming as eternal as these stars. As the priests performed the ceremony they recited: "You live again, you revive always, you have become young again, you are young again and forever."

WEIGHING THE HEART

The Weighing of the Heart is the Egyptian equivalent of Judgment Day, when a person's good and bad actions are weighed against each other. Egyptians believed that these actions were recorded in the heart. The heart was put on one side of a great scale and weighed against a sacred feather called Maat, which represents all truth, order, and rightness.

The monster god Amut, whose name means "devourer of the dead" and who was composed of parts of a hippo, lion, and crocodile, observed the weighing of the heart. He swallowed up anyone whose heart did not balance against truth.

Paintings depicting the Weighing of the Heart ceremony always show a happy ending. The deceased is pronounced "true of voice" and is led into the heavenly realm. Here, the Egyptians believed they would enjoy eternal life in a world like Egypt, but without pain and suffering.

GODS AND TEMPLES

The ancient Egyptians worshiped thousands of gods and goddesses, who were human, animal, or

This great symbol of the goddess Hathor marks a chapel at Hatshepsut's temple.

part human and part animal. Different aspects of a god's personality could be represented by different animals.

The Egyptian gods can be divided into local gods, national gods, and universal gods. Egypt was divided into forty-two districts, and each had its own local god, traditions, and customs. Amun, for example, was the local god of the city and region of Thebes. Osiris was the god of Abydos, Hathor of Dendera, and Ptah of Memphis.

Often these local gods were regarded as part of a divine family, consisting of a couple and their child. This formed a group of three, or a triad. One such triad is Osiris, Isis, and Horus; another is Amun, his wife Mut, and their child Khonsu.

When a major Egyptian city became the capital city, its local god became known and was worshiped nationally. During the Old Kingdom, when the capital was Memphis, Ptah was important throughout the country. Similarly, in the New Kingdom, when Thebes was the capital, temples and shrines to Amun were erected everywhere.

Universal gods and goddesses represent universal phenomena such as the sun, moon, sky, air, or moisture, and did not necessarily come from a specific region of ancient Egypt.

THE CREATION MYTH

Nine gods play key roles in the most popular myth of the creation of the world. The sun god, Ra (pronounced rah), created order from the chaos of the elements of water, air, earth, and sky. He created a pair of deities by spitting: Shu, god of air and light, and Tefnut, goddess of moisture.

Shu and Tefnut created the space between the earth and the sky. This couple produced two children: Geb, god of earth, and Nut, the sky goddess. They, in turn, had four children named Osiris, Isis, Seth, and Nepthys. Together, these nine gods formed what was called the ennead (the Greek word for nine) of the town Heliopolis. Heliopolis was chosen because it is the traditional home of the sun god Ra.

THE MYTH OF ISIS AND OSIRIS

Many versions of the myth of Isis and Osiris exist. Essentially, however, the story is as follows.

Osiris became the first king of Egypt; Isis was his wife. Their evil brother Seth murdered Osiris. Isis

This sculpture of Horus was made during the Ptolemaic Dynasty, when the pharaohs of Egypt were Greek.

and Nepthys managed to revive Osiris long enough for him to father a child with Isis. The child, Horus, became heir to the throne. In a battle with his uncle Seth he lost an eye but killed his father's murderer. Horus became king on earth, and Osiris became the king of all the gods in the next world.

Every king who took the throne of Egypt was compared to the good and triumphant king Horus, and was even called "The Horus." When people died they were called "The Osiris," and compared to Osiris, because everyone hoped to live eternally like Osiris. It is rare to find a coffin, stela, or tomb inscription that does not have the name or the image of one or all of the gods of this myth.

TEMPLES

Most Egyptian temples were built to honor a particular god. The spirit of the god was believed to live in the statue of the god that was housed in the sacred chamber, or sanctuary, at the back of the temple. Only priests and royalty had access to this sacred area. Most Egyptians could not even enter the temple—they worshiped outside the walls or, during special festivals, were allowed into the first inner courtyard.

A temple complex consisted of many buildings, including dwellings for the priests and many workshops to create everything that a god might need, ranging from linen-weaving workshops to bakeries. Under King Ramesses II, for example, the temple of Amun in Thebes employed 81,322 people and owned 433 gardens, 924 square miles of fields,

One of the most famous temples in Egypt is that of Amun-Ra at Karnak. The columns of this great hall were erected during the 19th Dynasty, under Sety I and Ramesses II.

83 boats, 46 construction yards, and 65 small market towns. All these things were to insure that the god was well cared for and properly worshiped.

WAKING THE GOD

Daily worship in Egypt's temples was based on the belief that the spirit of the god had to return to his or her statue in the sanctuary with each dawn. In theory, only the godlike pharaoh could look upon the face of a god. But since the king could not be present at every temple, he appointed a high-ranking priest at each temple to perform his duties for him.

At dawn the high priest broke the clay seal on the door of the shrine that held the god's statue. He removed the candle from the previous day and lit a new one. At the exact moment that the sun appeared on the horizon, he removed the sculpture from its shrine, and recited: "I have seen the god. The god rejoices at seeing me. I have gazed upon the statue."

Then the leading chanter sang the morning hymn to awaken the power of the god in the statue:

You have risen, you are in peace; rise beautifully in peace; wake, you god of this city, to life!

The gods were worshiped many times during the day, but the first time was at sunrise.

Your eyes cast a flame!
Your eyes illuminate the night!
Your brows wake in beauty!
O radiant face!

Once the god's power was present, the priest, bowing in an attitude of respect, prayed toward the north, east, south, and west, spreading his prayer to every corner of the world. The finest food and drink offerings from the temple estate were placed before the statue of the god. After a specified amount of time had passed, the priests removed what the god had not spiritually "eaten." They divided the

A painted relief carving of the pharaoh Sety I making an offering of food to one of the gods

offering among themselves, so they ate like gods too.

The priests washed the god's statue, put new linen around it, and anointed the statue with sacred oils. The high priest put oil on the little finger of his right hand, then touched it to the brow of the divine statue. The statue was then returned to its shrine. As the priests left the sanctuary they burned incense to purify the air and swept away any traces of their footsteps in the sand.

ASTRONOMERS AND ASTROLOGERS

The Egyptians kept very precise records of time. Timekeepers tended the great granite water clocks that kept time through the night when the sun's position could not be measured. Astronomers studied the planets and stars to determine when religious holidays and festivals should start. Astrologers predicted which days were lucky, neutral, or unlucky.

SCHOLARS

Each major temple had a department called The House of Life, which was a center for scholarly thought. Here scribes copied religious and technical documents and prepared textbooks. The temple library, called the House of Books, housed the great papyrus scrolls on every subject. Unfortunately, very few of these precious scrolls have survived.

The Egyptians were known throughout the ancient world as experts on religion, history, geography, astronomy, geometry, herbal medicine, and the diagnosis and treatment of diseases. Many famous Greek philosophers studied at Egyptian temples, including Plato, who studied geometry and religion in Egypt for thirteen years.

EVERYDAY LIFE

We know a great deal about what life was like in ancient Egypt, thanks to the discovery of thousands of objects from that time as well as the art work and writings of the Egyptians themselves.

HOUSES

The ancient Egyptians—like many modern Egyptians today—lived in flat-roofed houses made of mud bricks. Bricks were shaped by packing a mixture of mud and straw into rectangular wooden molds. The wet bricks were left in the sun to dry.

After a mud brick house was built, its walls were covered with white plaster, and the floors were

A golden chair from Tutankhamun's tomb

often covered with reed mats. The hot weather dictated the design of the house. The windows were small and very high up, which kept out the sun and dust. Most houses had stairs going up to a roof terrace, where the family could sit at night and host celebrations. Egyptian houses were cool and fresh.

FURNITURE

Wealthier families owned fine wooden chairs that still look surprisingly modern. Other households had only reed stools. A successful official might have a fine wooden bed with a woven leather mattress; a poor person slept on a mat on the floor. A wooden headrest—rather than a pillow—was used for sleeping. Instead of cupboards and bureaus, Egyptians used small wooden chests and covered baskets.

FOOD

Egyptian farmers grew barley and wheat. From these crops they made bread and beer—the two staples of the Egyptian diet. Vegetables eaten in Egypt included onions, garlic, leeks, cucumbers, lentils, and lettuce. Fruits included dates, figs, pomegranates, and grapes.

Wealthier Egyptians regularly ate meat from oxen, sheep, goats, ducks, and geese. The average family ate mostly fish, beans, and eggs for protein. For dessert, they baked fancy cakes in spiral, animal, or human shapes, and flavored them with honey, sesame, or dates.

Foods were stored in pottery containers, oils were placed in vessels with small necks made for pouring, and grains and flours were stored in larger jars. Fish and duck were dried and placed in these jars, which were then sealed to preserve the meat.

SONG AND DANCE

Upper-class Egyptians are pictured in paintings on tomb walls enjoying banquets, and we know that the average person celebrated many religious festivals and family celebrations. Guests were entertained by small groups of musicians playing the harp, lyre, lute, and flute. Dancers accompanied them, playing tambourines and clappers like castanets and sometimes even performing acrobatics. Judging from these instruments, early Egyptian music was probably soft and soothing. Unfortunately, the musical notes were never written down, so the exact sound is not known.

PERSONAL APPEARANCE

The Egyptians were concerned with personal cleanliness and appearance. Wealthier homes had shallow baths where the owners stood while their servants

This relief carving from a noble's tomb portrays his sister. Her hair is beautifully styled, and she wears eye makeup typical of ancient Egypt.

poured water over them. Egyptian men and women rubbed scented oils on their skin to combat the hot, dusty climate. Both sexes owned sets of copper or brass razors and tweezers, which they used to remove body hair. The men were generally clean-shaven, although they sometimes wore a thin mustache.

Men and women applied eye makeup made of ground minerals mixed with water. Pigments from a copper ore called malachite made green eye paint, and lead ore, known as galena, made black. The outlines around their eyes made them look large and beautiful, but the paints also contained medicinal properties that helped prevent eye disease, which was common due to wind-blown dust particles.

Women wore lipcolor and rouge made from berries and minerals, such as red ocher. Their mirrors were polished brass disks. A wealthy person might have a silver disk for a mirror.

Egyptians spent a lot of time on their hair, as demonstrated by the many wigs, braids, false curls, combs, hair curlers, and hairpins that have been found in tombs. Hair fashions changed rapidly, especially during the New Kingdom. Hairstyles worn in tomb paintings of 1500 B.C., for example, were out of fashion by 1450 B.C.

All Egyptians wore clothing of linen, which was made from the flax plant. The clothing found in tombs shows that the working classes sometimes wore simple knee-length linen tunics or loincloths of linen or leather. Women generally wore long dresses. They could be close fitting with wide shoulder straps, which was a classic design of the Old Kingdom, or full dresses draped and tied at the front,

Egyptian women usually wore long dresses, as seen in this painted relief carving of a woman named Hapy.

which were popular in the New Kingdom. Men wore pleated or plain kilts, which could be long or short, close fitting or triangular shaped. In some periods the kilt was worn with a tight linen shirt or shawl.

When dressing for a celebration, wealthy Egyptians anointed themselves with expensive, perfumed oils and wore their finest linens and a highly styled, curled wig. When they arrived at the banquet, servants placed wide collars made of leaves, petals, and berries on their necks. Cones of scented wax that melted down over their hair and shoulders, coloring them yellow and creating a pleasant perfume, were also placed on their heads.

WRITING AND ART

It is fortunate that writing and art were so important in ancient Egypt. It is through these activities that we know so much about Egyptian civilization.

WRITING

The Egyptians' own name for their writing was "Words of the Gods." The word *hieroglyph* is a Greek word meaning "sacred carving."

The ancient Egyptians who learned to read and write were called scribes, and they learned their craft in special training schools. A scribe was most likely from a middle-class family that could afford the luxury of sending a child to school, the ancient equivalent of a college education. The scribe could then get a respected job in Egyptian society.

It took years to learn to be a scribe. They learned more than seven hundred signs. Each was a picture of an object, animal, or person. But hieroglyphs are not simply picture writing. Some signs represent a sound or combination of sounds. Other signs are visual aids that help understand the words—for example, a picture of legs to illustrate the word "run."

Hieroglyphs can be written right to left, left to right, or top to bottom and are generally read toward the faces of the humans or animals in the signs.

Most Egyptian art was created in honor of gods or placed in Egyptian tombs because of the belief that the art objects would come alive in the afterlife.

To help them come to life, objects and persons are carved or painted in great detail. In drawing a figure, every body part is shown from its clearest point of view. The face is drawn from the side to show the profile, but the eye is drawn from the front, to reveal its familiar outline. The shoulders are drawn from the front, but the legs from the side. These combinations of views are what make Egyptian art unique and life-like, although they are not true to nature.

Also, the Egyptians did not draw closer objects larger and farther ones smaller as we do. They made

In Egyptian art each part of the body is drawn from the angle that makes it most recognizable. Notice how the faces and feet of the figures are in profile but their shoulders are frontal.

the more important people and things larger than the less important: a servant, for example, would be drawn half the size of his or her master or mistress.

EGYPTIAN ARTISTS

Egyptian artists did not work alone, but in a group. Each artist was a specialist in one part of the production process.

A relief carving on a wall, for example, would be made in a sequence of steps: First an artist would draw an outline of the scene in black paint, then a master outliner would correct this work in red ink. A sculptor who was skilled at working with a chisel would chip away the large areas of stone from around the drawing. A master carver would create the finer features of the sculpture. Finally, a painter would color the sculpture and paint in such details as jewelry, clothing, and hairstyles.

The artists almost always showed the Egyptians in stiff poses. Because Egyptian art was created for a temple or tomb, the figures were shown in a serious, religious mood.

Though figures in Egyptian art do not show emotion, such Egyptian love poetry as the following example makes it clear that Egyptians were often very warm and loving to each other:

I shall not leave you,
My hand is in your hand;
You and I shall wander in all the places fair.

The art and writing of ancient Egypt have allowed its legacy to live on. In a way, they have made ancient Egyptian civilization immortal—as immortal as ancient Egyptians believed they themselves would be, and as immortal as the ideas contained in this blessing from ancient Egypt: "May you rise like the sun, rejuvenate yourself like the moon, and repeat life like the flood of the Nile."

TIMELINE

2920–2575 B.C.	Early Dynastic Period (Dynasties 1–3)
2575–2134	Old Kingdom (Dynasties 4–6)
	Dynasty 4 (2575–2465 B.C.)
	Pharaoh Chufu (2551–2528 B.C.)
2134–2040	First Intermediate Period (Dynasties 9–10)
2040–1640	Middle Kingdom (Dynasties 11–14)
1649–1532	Second Intermediate Period (Dynasties 15–17)
1550–1070	New Kingdom (Dynasties 18–20)
	Dynasty 18 (1550–1307 B.C.)
	Pharaoh Hatshepsut (1473-1458 B.C.)
	Pharaoh Tutankhamun (1333–1323 B.C.)
	Dynasty 19 (1307–1196 B.C.)
	Pharaoh Ramesses II (1290–1224 B.C.)
1070–712	Third Intermediate Period (Dynasties 21–25)
712–332	Late Period (Dynasties 26–30)
332–30	Greek and Ptolemaic Rule
	Pharaoh Cleopatra (51–30 B.C.)
30 B.C.–A.D. 395	Roman Rule

GLOSSARY

afterlife existence after death

alabaster fine-textured white stone

amulet small religious object or figure believed to provide magical protection for its wearer

cataracts fierce rapids formed by granite boulders in the Nile

dynasty rule of a country by one family for an extended period of time

excavation process of digging away at the earth to expose remains buried underground

harem group of women associated with one man

hieroglyphs characters of the Egyptian system of writing

Intermediate Period break between dynasties in ancient Egypt when warring or neighboring countries ruled

obelisk upright, four-sided pillar that tapers to a pyramid

quarry area where building stone can be excavated

relief carving shallow carving on a flat stone surface

shendjet short, pleated kilt that was part of the traditional Egyptian pharaoh costume

uraeus rearing cobra worn on the forehead of the pharaoh, a typical symbol of kingship

FOR FURTHER READING

Hart, George. *Ancient Egypt*. Eyewitness Books. New York: Knopf, 1990.

National Geographic. *Ancient Egypt: Discovering Its Splendors*. Washington, DC: National Geographic Society, 1978.

FOR ADVANCED READERS

Andrews, Carol. *Egyptian Mummies*. Cambridge: Harvard University Press, 1984.

Robbins, Gay. *Women in Ancient Egypt*. London: British Museum Press, 1993.

WEB SITES

Due to the changeable nature of the Internet, sites appear and disappear very quickly. Internet addresses must be entered with capital and lowercase letters exactly as they appear.

Carnegie Museum of Natural History—Life in Ancient Egypt: http://www.clpgh.org/cmnh/tours/egypt/walton.html

Ancient Egypt page: http://www.pcola.gulf.net/~anubis/

Your Mining Co. Guide to Ancient/Classical History: http://ancienthistory.miningco.com/msub9.htm

INDEX

A
Abu Simbel, 30–31
afterlife, 10, 27–28, 57
Akhenaton, 23–25
Alexander the Great, 31
Alexandria, 31, 32
Amenhotep, 23
Amun, 39, 42–43
Amut, 37
Anubis, 35–36
appearance, personal, 51–55
architecture, 10, 22
art, Egyptian, 10, 25, 57–59
Aswan dam, 9
Aton, 25

B
ba (human mind/ bodily ability), 34, 35
beer, 19, 50

C
Caesar, Julius, 32
Carter, Howard, 27
cataracts, 9, 30
Champollion, Jean François, 13

Chufu, pharaoh, 17–19
Cleopatra VII, 31–33
coffins, Tutankh- amun's, 28
costume, pharaohs', 20, 32
creation, myth of, 40
culture, Egyptian, 10, 12, 17

D
Deir el Bahri, 20
desert, 6, 9, 22
dynasty, 9–10, 17, 31–32

E
ennead, 40
entertainment, 51

F
flooding, Nile, 6
food, 50–51

G
Geb, 40
Giza, pyramids at, 17–18
gods, 10, 27, 37–46
gold, 10, 27, 28
Greeks, 10, 12, 17, 31

H
hairstyles, 53, 55
Hathor, 39
Hatshepsut, pharaoh, 19–23, 32
heart, weighing of, 37
hieroglyphs, 10, 12–13, 56–57
Horus, 39, 41–42
houses, 48–49

I
Intermediate Periods, 10, 15
Isis, 39, 40–41

J
jewelry, 27–28

K
ka (human vital force), 34, 35
Karnak, 15

L
Luxor, 15

M
makeup, 52–53
Marc Antony, 32
Middle Kingdom, 15

mummification,
27–28, 35

N
Nepthys, 40–41
New Kingdom, 15,
17, 27, 39, 53,
55
Nile River, 6–9, 12
Nubia, 12, 17, 29
Nut, 40

O
obelisk, 23
Octavian, 32
Old Kingdom, 15,
39, 53
opening of mouth
ceremony, 35–36
Osiris, 39, 40–41, 42

P
pharaohs, 9–10, 14–33
power, passing of,
9–10, 31–32

priests, 15, 42–46
Ptah, 39
Ptolemy I, 31
Ptolemy XV
Caesarion, 32
pyramids, 14, 17,
18–19, 27

R
Ra, 40
Ramesses II, 29–31,
42–44
relief carvings, 22,
58–59
religion, 10, 14, 34–37
Romans, 12, 17, 32
Rosetta Stone, 13
rulers, foreign, 15,
31–33

S
shendjet (kilt), 20,
32, 55
Shu, 40

T
Tefnut, 40
temple, 12, 14–15,
19, 20, 30–31,
42–46, 59
Thebes, 27, 39, 42
Thutmose II, III,
19–20, 23
tombs, royal, 14, 19,
27, 57, 59
Tutankhamun,
25–29

V
Valley of the Kings,
14, 26

W
women pharaohs,
19, 32–33
worship, daily,
44–46
writing, 10, 56–57

ABOUT THE AUTHOR

Egyptologist Joyce Haynes is the author of five books and many scholarly articles on ancient Egypt and Nubia. A consultant in the department of Ancient Egyptian, Nubian, and Near Eastern Art at the Museum of Fine Arts, Boston, she also teaches Egyptian art and hieroglyphs.